carbon-dating hunger

by
Anthony Seidman

The Bitter Oleander Press
Fayetteville, New York 13066-9776

2000

BITTER OLEANDER
P R E S S

The Bitter Oleander Press
4983 Tall Oaks Drive
Fayetteville, New York 13066-9776
USA

Manufactured in the United States of America

Printed by McNaughton & Gunn, Inc.
Saline, Michigan

Cover Design & Layout:
Roderick Martinez Visual Communications
Liverpool, New York

ISBN #: 0-9664358-1-8

Library of Congress Catalog Card Number: 99-97288

The following journals are gratefully acknowledged in which some of these poems
first appeared:

California Quarterly: Making the Pact Outside Chihuahua, Vermeer, Xipe la segunda
Cider Press Review: Chihuahua Desert. *Códice (Mexico City):* The Uncapped Pen
Luna: When Singing Doesn't Have To Be a Song, Fable of a Wolf, a Lyre, &
One Million Inhabitants
Hunger: Elementary. *Pinyon Poetry:* Listening to Ives' "The Unanswered Question
Rhino, Poetry Forum: In 2300 BC, Emperor Yao, On DeKooning's Woman I
The Bitter Oleander: Reaching the Step that Doesn't Crumble, Saying Goodbye to
Carthage, Yucatán, Poetry, The Cork which Floats on Water is Consumed by Flame
Tierra Adentro (Mexico City): Two
Sulphur River Literary Review: Like a Jutted Tooth I Stood

For Daniel & Ruth

With special thanks to Dominique Arnould

TABLE OF CONTENTS

The Stretched Canvas

All Things Inchoate

Language, Mortal Clay

TAKING THE UNKNOWN ROAD: *The Poetry of Anthony Seidman*

It's appropriate that a brand new voice would emerge with the millennium. Especially a voice whose language excites and then compels us to absorb a huge range of textures, objects, colors, places, scents and their associations in and out of a relationship with them all. Anthony Seidman comes out of a rejected tradition of sense for the sake of popular appeal and grows within an imaginative landscape whose language, by necessity of all he's experienced, constructs the definition of each of his poems-to-be. Never trying to complete a poem, his work seems always in a state of progress.

As we read his poems, everything in our world comes apart. We no longer have the same expectations of reality that we once had. Objects become animated beyond our expectations. They are allowed to rendez-vous with other objects in associative combinations that, though previously unthought of, once joined, seem to be a necessity to each other. Through this allowance for the unexpected, Seidman has created a poetry of infinite proportions, depicting a time in his life where the dust and sun enriched tortillas of Juárez filled his veins full of poverty, hunger, love, misery, and lust. Yet, embedded in his wide-open eyes, he sees no other choice but to write it out, not only to its fullest expression, but to its most imaginative portrayal via a language raw with its own life and his passion.

All most of us ever see in our daily lives, has very little to do with the reality we get to glimpse through Seidman's eyes. We may share the riches of a common language, but the words he chooses to speak, easily surpass our seemingly mundane expectations of them. To read him, you must allow yourself to live differently, breathe differently, intuit and think differently, and sometimes have your heart beat in a most unfamiliar rhythm the way a mountain lion's stride might glide while pursuing a snowshoe hare or within the persistence of Monarch butterfly wings rising to migrate higher above an even more powerful wind.

Today's poetry demands its poets to be over-productive, to fill vast notebooks with publishable, decent material. The sudden cyber-spaciality that's now arrived to encumber our lives even further with everyone elses', will make an even greater demand on the ordinary to appear special. The ensuing subjectivity, its self-centeredness and generalized truth-telling that accompanies it, will no longer act as that representative of the consciousness existing in our interiors as human beings. That part of us then will be lost, will be terrorized by a state of mind that dictates, repeats, and shares the same truths while simultaneously stunting the perception of every treasured but unseen event happening around us. Which makes it all the more important for us to have someone like Seidman, whose total perception expands the vision of the details we easily and unfortunately lose sight of in our day-to-day lives.

How he does this is not so simple. He does not make it up as he goes along. Experiences string together with bursts of magnesium light and the city, the countryside, the body of a woman, the cantina and the street gutters are all seen in the brilliance of their own selves, totally unencumbered by each's usual meaning or reference point. Everything becomes what it already is. Everything speaks from a place in which we feel like we've been before but without having realized it at the time. Seidman simply refuses to depend on anything he knows. His entrance into each experience is as a complete alien and what he sees is exactly what is there, not at all what he brings with him as docent or interpreter.

Freeing his language to unfold the feelings he has about what his life contacts, allows him to move in uncharted rivers full of swift currents and unpredictable turns. He handles each approach well. He's careful never to overwhelm his imagery with the sediment of embellishment thus causing the poem to beach on a sandbar or rock shore. Nor are there any ornate targets that he feels he must possess, or truths expostulated that he thinks are his very own. Rather, there is a different truth revealed: the one that states the depths to which language can go in revealing a poet's soul in progress as it moves from the real to the surreal. Still, don't think this poetry requires a label. It is neither entirely Surrealist, nor Deep Imagist. It does not follow the pattern of the superconscious and yet it does have a revelatory value the way a raindrop contains an ocean.

What Seidman has recovered, and not by accident, is the tradition in poetry where language, its sound and most internalized meaning, has the ingenuity to render the once-feared emptiness of the page harmless and elevate the poet to a new height of consciousness. Where once the dictates of a highly rational poetry promulgated having the intent to write with purposeful meaning, purposeful phrasing, meter and rhyme as the rule rather than the exception, Seidman's work stands outside this limited approach to reality's thumbprint and instead demands attention be paid to the unexpected. At every turn, he coaxes and lures us with a music of words laid out in paths like precious stones.

Oddly enough, the trance, the spell under which we succumb, is self-induced. So captivated are we by Seidman's vision, that our own sense of language veritably transforms itself into his shapes and patterns and we see ourselves for the very first time in a most unique way. Because of his vision, we're watching grass grow over our faces just so mud can flow from our eyes each time we cry. Because of his vision, we feel birdfeathers socket in our armpits and flutter each time we raise our arms up in celebration of the total glee we experience because of our cozy predicament. Above all, we can finally be no one else but ourselves. We can set up paths that lead themselves as they unfold. How long we remain here, how long this ecstatic state of mind provides enough nourishment to propel our new vision, seems bound only by the duration which exists where our perception first enjoys this new view of ourselves. And we have Seidman to thank entirely for this, because it's his vision which has pushed the door a little more ajar for us, making it so we can enter where he's been waiting all along.

Paul B. Roth

Si hemos podido mapear un mundo de
tres dimensiones en dos, ha de ser
posible mapear un mundo de cuatro en tres

—Alberto Blanco

(If we've been able to map a world of
three dimensions in two, it must be
possible to map a world of four in three)

REACHING THE STEP THAT DOESN'T CRUMBLE

Between stars and bread,
between the click of a light switch
and the bulb's white flash,
between the taste of salt
and waves folding foam on the shore,
(around the bend of a coastal hill),
between this or that, and
between the between which resounds in this chant,
the cherry ripe in the brain,
the panting of a man running in his sleep,
fishnet swollen with a catch of air,
twig-snap thundering in a canyon,
and a basement perched on the shoulder,
and an attic rumbling in the stomach,
there is a word which can be peeled,
there is an odor sweet as a dead goat,
a color blinding as a lemon,
and all that passes through my brain
as I sit at this desk is like
a breath whirling between
5 o'clock and the universe,
where clouds litter leaves,
and a rain falls up from the earth to
plant swallows on the branches of this tree.

MAKING THE PACT OUTSIDE CHIHUAHUA

It was a busstop, and past midnight
at a 24 hour diner with smoke
basted on tile walls, and vats of pork
boiled in red chili sauce.
I stepped outside; light sped towards
me from stars and supernovas. A rust-
flavored wind stirred cobalt clouds,
and lightning cracked the night, struck
where sky meets earth, where black
touches black, and becomes neither.

XIPE LA SEGUNDA

(a photo by Manuel Alvarez Bravo)

Because a drop of water creates amoeba,
insectae floating in the embryo of their universe
and fish nipping at the edge
where water touches air but is neither,
because a drop of water turns into a lake,
because a drop of water is
the Milky Way and a water lily floats
and mud cools the shore,
your eyes rustle ferns
as you stare at Xipe the forever mother,
because you breathe,
and now step out into the light which at once,
turns from black and white into sunshine and
green shade beneath palm trees,
because you approach Xipe,
stretch-marked hips and her navel
the scar of two ripped apart,
because you will lie down with her,
and the eyes behind your chest will open,
and the sun inside her womb will rise,
because a man and a woman are a drop of water,
because Xipe is sex fusing with sex,
because Xipe is stone striking sparks against stone,
she hands you her dress to toss on the ground,
as lizards sun themselves then scatter,
and lianas curl around the bough.

GOD TORMENTS THE BARREN ONCE AGAIN

—after Joaquín Pasos

Evening in Juárez. The cantinas are empty.
A taxi stuffed with American soldiers crackles over gravel.
It is the hour of the leaf-swirl
when homeowners lock their doors and
the childless, aging young woman
steps out into the street,
rips open her blouse so that
the wind will hone her breasts like volcanoes.

POETRY

—after Amir Gilboa

Light of lost suns pours through my fingers because
You are cloud, stone, and smoke I eat,
You are altar where blood is drained from goat and liturgy.
Suns of lost lights open my fingers because
You are a tower of cinnamon toppled by my tongue;
I enter You and You swallow my fish and amber glow.
Forest slides over me, wheat bristles on thighs of wind;
Oh Voice scaled like a wall of water, Oh
Sap lacquered over the wood of my song.
Open me and leaves scatter over the buried virgin;
Enter me, impale me, pluck me from buds of fire;
From the wounds You inflict moons are spawned.
When You open Your legs I swallow the sun.

I WILL SAIL TO SANTO DOMINGO ONE DAY

—to Amaury Terrero, after so many invitations

On a ship lighter than the first word uttered in the jungle. Boatswains will bob by my keel in green phosphorescence, jettisoned tigers will spit electric fish, and the wind will smell of fluid mushrooms and blue flowers. To be far from where snow crusts pine, and the oak bleeds in autumn. Stalactites will chew my heart as reefs bare their teeth. Flowers will bloom gangrenous on the water, as night bleeds slow hemlock. I will hear the singing that melts wax, and for which sailors kiss the moon-slick on the sea. Dawns will taste of egg cracked on raw meat as the sun will begin its descent to the precipice of the blue abyss. I will sail to Santo Domingo on a ship made of words, for a port of tar and tamarind, where water cools in clay jars, and each mango is a miniature sun.

LISTENING TO IVES' *THE UNANSWERED QUESTION*

Over the iron-furnace roar
of a jet flying through
clouds dragging water which falls
down on these chaparral and oak hills as
roads are slickened into snake skin,
and over rain bobbing leaves,
over the drizzle,
over the shape of clouds like
cigarette smoke exhaled under water,
the jet has now passed,
leaving that sound softer than
silk sheets rustling beneath blankets,
that sound silent between
the orchestra tuned and the conductor's
baton poised in midair—
it is a violin drawing out a chord
which pulls the ocean's weight when
the tide is pregnant with the moon,
it is the question which severs brain
from spirit and spirit from breath
while an oboe pierces a sphere where
no bird has flown,
it is the question for which light
is carved out of black water,
and aspic invertebrates flash
from the depths in a glass of water, then die,
it is the question which blasts trumpets
while here, the drizzle continues,
and leaves drown in their greenness.

TWO

1

Mosquito, the hours
you live suffice.
Moon without wings.

2

Blue blue of the sky, radiantly coquettish—
When I stretch up I feel you just within reach.

THE UNCAPPED PEN

Between these words is a jungle: lianas coil around a stone deity, half-serpent, half-whore, with granite hummingbird feathers as a crown, and clawed feet. Gnats, mosquitos, and shade bullet-shot from white sun-rays, and the humid stink, like the feet of cheese vendors in the market. Every frond of palms I brush open reveals a cliff's edge, and at the bottom, clouds roll slowly, dragging unfallen rain. The deity sometimes speaks to me, here, at the peak of the tropical Himalaya. Drums, drums, I beat but no clouds reach me. I decipher this jungle stone by stone because only the myopic can gaze into the star beneath the sun. Lianas move in wind and stroke her granite thighs. Drums, drums, I beat, waiting for rains to word. When they fall, the sun bursts in another hemisphere, frost thaws, and a hiss escapes from her granite mouth—a wordless prayer for the jungle between words.

JEWEL OF THIRST

The door of fire is a harpsichord of blood.
The door of fire is palm leaves laid supplicant at the hooves of a goat.
The door of fire is hope in a maguey thorn.
The door of fire is a needle threading water through the eye of a camel.
But you are a door of fire with your stomach of wheat,
You with your tongue of mud,
You with your fingers of rain,
You with an ax splitting open the sun,
You with your feet of milk,
With your breasts of ivy,
With your eyebrows that rustle at night and weave a frond for the moon,
With your eyes the color of a lion's mane.
Oh world forever eaten by thirst,
The door of fire is water, and
Words brimming with a sky no birds contain.
Oh thirst never slaked by life,
The door of fire is Time that spawns, suckles, then devours me.

YUCATÁN

The road to Yucatán stretches
    between an ant's
    bread-crumb burden
    and a ripe melon,
    between the moon frozen
    at noon, and the stone
    that bakes in my palm,
    through the sun that
    rises from under my shadow
    and is peeled in an onion.

To taste the Yucatán:
    ferns and palm trees in
    the yawn of a spider,
    fanatical whims of the hummingbird,
    a fruit cart painted lime, a mule
    with a hardon, milk
    in the sponge, and
    a mouthful of wasps.

But the road to Yucatán is only
    the road.

The road to Yucatán is
    feather, bean,
    vine, and dust;

the road to Yucatán is
    indelibly indelibly
    erased

from a map drafted tomorrow.

FABLE FOR THE LIVING

The dead hoist stars
with rope woven from
oil-bleed of sunken tankers.
The stalight is a silver
cool to the touch as
salamander skin, if
only you could touch them,
(or see them).
The dead spoon-scrape
cans of chili while riding in
flooded boxcars creaking
through fields of smoke.
Sluices carve
the buried bones they no longer kiss;
they know that a range
of stumps is the darkest forest,
and that to proceed
with the chess game is ludicrous:
eyes of slaughtered ewes stare
from the black squares,
and razors gleam in the white.
No more music, no haiku,
the dead have burned the map,
and chuckle as you iron, drink, or
figure the speed of photons while
the weight of light topples the tower.
Because the dead bet on when
the bridge will fall, on when the last
human cell will shrivel
in mid-mitosis.
And they are studying you,
a mere column of blood
that melts
from four corners of wind
like an ice-cube in the mouth.

La sospechosamente siempreverdeante Soar

—Carlos Martínez Rivas

(The suspiciously evergreening Zohar)

I COME FROM THE TRIBE OF CLOUDS

My words pour
sleet or fire.

The earth is hard
but below me.

WOOD

In my grain you touch
holes where light is fossilized,
maps of blood,
and the caravan of water across
sands where rain sizzles on roofs.
In my bark you study shapes
suggesting hunchback and hyena, the wind
banging shutters of an empty house.
I am what the mirror would
reveal if that face
staring back would blink first.
I am the desire you carve,
the keel of an argosy
slicing flotsam. I am your words,
flotilla set sail for Florida
and fountain of rejuvenation!
While your pen
inks paper, while you sit
at this desk, you forget
sweet smell of Lebanese cedar,
mahogany mud-stink
of Nicaraguan jungles, the crack
of a wind-split oak, and twigs
snapping underfoot in
your journey from pit to
fruit and light. You forget
I am not the modus:
I am your want, the open-
arm embrace, & the three rusted nails.

I am the memory of the garden before it bloomed.
I am the garden devoured with one bite, red pulp-juice on my sleeve.
I am earth dug by men who learned to turn their arms into shovels to
        unearth a toothless jawbone.
I am Joshua trees dying at the desert's edge where an interstate splits open
        the first darkness.
At night the interstate asphalt glows like the wet, barnacled skin of a
        sperm whale plunging beneath waves.
By day, dust and the buzzing of cars, mosquito whine of motorcycles, and
        howling 18 wheelers loaded with skinned cows and frozen lettuce.
Midnight,
and I am a car speeding down the interstate.
Miles beneath my shaking chassis are rivers of molten nickel and iron.
Miles above my roof, air reaching cooler air, sheet-haze of smog, ultraviolet
        light, and then the All Empty one could cap inside a Coke bottle.
I am the map of the interstate and of all interstates, cardiovascular veins
        wound into a ball.
I am the memory of the map before the map was drawn.
A Mobil station burns red neon, Pegasus kicks in midflight, and newspapers
        blow past the pumps.
The first billboard flashes past my windshield.
I am the smoke from a cigarette lit inside that car and
I am the man coughing who downshifts, headlights glowing on an exit sign.
And I drive down a street lined with town houses.
Dogs bark at the sight of my car the way a prophet points to a comet.
At last I pull into a driveway where insomniac crickets chirp,
and I stretch in front of my door, and take a deep breath.
Home is where I started.

WHERE SOURCE AND SHADOW ARE FUSED

To travel at the speed of light
you must become sun chafed
under the weight of a stone,
air glistening in a rope
of water poured from a clay jug,
and noon's sizzling flash on
cars rattling over potholes.
It is not enough to harvest
protein from a plum, gather
desire from the sandaled feet
of a woman across the aisle on a bus,
and reach the speed where angles
of a square become round, and
a circle is the straightest line
to reach where source
and shadow are fused. To travel
at the velocity of moonlight,
and with the ardor of crab-nebulae,
you must learn how to
inhale water, and drown in
that black liquidity when
the ladder of milk had just
reached your lair of sexless
hydrogen and dust. Only then,
like the flitting of the hummingbird,
whir of atoms unlocking in granite,
grumble of shifting faults erasing
your glimpse of the earth's homecoming
from molten core into helium cloud, only
then will you learn: light pulls you from sleep
so that together you knock down
these great walls of static and meat.

ENZYME

Get it from Muddy Waters howling *I'm the Hoochie Coochie Man*;
you can get it too
from chewing of mouthful of blue electricity.
I get it from a slash of De Kooning yellow blind my dream of suburban Havana;
get it from cold water during Juárez dog days,
from the thrill of peeling an orange;
get it from blood-gut in the stomach of a mosquito—

the enzyme kicking open brain-doors for the upchuck of genius.
Feeling the wind which spins this earth,
tumult of the thunder night,
scarlet the mind spits when a woman spreads.

I digest the enzyme, I am changed:
A jolt cracks my skull and
smacks open the curtains
to let in the sun.

ELEMENTARY

If of all acids milk is the blackest,
and the cargo of blue roses drifts
beyond the longitude of language;
if the joys of adultery pin
a wet doormat on the horse's hoof,
and semen
curdles in ovaries of a burning bush—
that can only mean
midnight has struck on the tower clock
and a mesh of oily
shadows slink over the plaza tiles.
In the distance, a girl in a ribboned
straw hat waits at the dock,
while a cruiser belches smoke.
There is no voyage
without the compass and the pole,
no vowels without the hermeticism of carbon,
no altars without the torched orchard,
and though claws may catch on the tiger's smile,
of all truths
to which you must adhere,
never trap a moth between two windows.

CHIHUAHUA DESERT

First Vision

Believe that granite is soluble, that
prickly pear yearns for skin and teeth.
Believe chaparral blooms in the brain when
rain wears a cracked arroyo. Believe
jackrabbit scurries over sand to sniff
jagged strips of night, and that these
words sweat dust, that the sky
pours indigo over the desert while
the moon calcifies your thirst.

Second Vision

This is the death of wind,
this is the bone of prayer and taste of tin—
here, thorn pierces the tongue of water,
teeth of dust chews cactus and weed,
heat secretes an enamel shell, heat
lays its eggs in the granite of sand,
here, sky is the bluest shade of fire,
and dew is the fourth mystery
in transubstantiation.

THE NILE

The terrible length of the Nile,
that broad-back flow through blue heat
and shore-line of gnat mud, ox dung,
and naked boys bathing in algae-sludge, and mothers
singing as they wade waist-deep
into the river. To taste
that water would be sweeter than all
the mezcal of Canada corked inside
the piss bottle of a Juárez Diva. The Nile,
a woman giving birth, ready for the meat hook,
feet in stirrups, womb lips
spread by rubber gloves of a doctor
tearing out a babe with teeth and
Krishna-blue skin.

When will I raise my anchor and sail
into that water bit all day by mosquitos,
river-top tense like the skin of a flea-rotten dog?
What will the Nile throw up?
What the shadows under my feet dissolve
when exposed to the sun. What my pencil traces in mid-air
but can never draft on paper.
I want the Nile to exhale a fly-swarm and blacken
my mind now lit, a glass of water
on a bleached table cloth. I want the Nile to be
a liqueur spiced with a pound of African sand so I can
savor how the purple of India, the pink of Bolivia, the ecru
of Madagascar were not the atlas pages
I thumbed while picking my nose during summer afternoons.

I thought the world would taste of stamps
I pasted on envelopes and sent to jungles and dazzling
shores, and which were never answered
while my mail box blazed a thousand suns!

When I sail through that delta
when my keel slices into the Nile,
my lover will no longer lick my ear
through the telephone, my enemy will no longer eat
my privacy, and my mother will never light the matches
wedged under my toenails. At last
I will sing the few tears on the apple,
a saxophone wailing at night, and a waterfall
switching on and off like a light bulb.

Alone with no recommendations
in the vast desert

—Yehuda Amichai

INTO THE THINNING SUMMER

STRIKING A MAJOR CHORD BETWEEN HEART & SOLE

As I collapse, shivering joy from
orgasm, the meat and water I am
continues wearing away until,
in fifty or seventy years,
nothing but a row of molars
on a jawbone and a skull
to last a millennium.
                                    But
there is a grumble of tectonic plates
that I do not hear, a molten
subterranean
ocean of nickel, iron, & copper.
                              There is
the noiseless burst of the sprout-
ing bean, and papyrus
rattling dryly by that
river where crocodile and man mated,
there is a mango that I
have never peeled with my quick,
white teeth.
                  That does not
offer consolation, nor is a prayer
for my swirl into the whirlpool, but
in the evening
when couples mate with
such fury that the
wind must split them apart,
and machinery of earth
grinds from dusk
to night, a breath
dissolves me with
semblance of siesta or tea,
and I lie down with my wife while
the first finger of moon stirs
the bedroom mirror from
sleep into a fathomless well.

IN 2300 BC, EMPEROR YAO

Beheaded
royal ministers Ho & Hi
because
drunk with courtesans
behind rice-paper screens
they forgot
to warn their Lord of
an eclipse.
           Thus
in the thinning
summer, I write
between steel-blue sky
and sand where tarantulas breed,
and search
for an omen that
will fix the moon
with the roaming, black
dog of my heart.

NOON

I was born at noon—
two great thighs and womb heaving me into the world, like the
force of a Viking village shoulder-hauling a ship into a foaming sea.
I was born at noon.
An oven-child of heat and sun flash on a tin roofed border town
where hot buses roar; the hour when shadows are appendix-thin and burst
as afternoon falls, when heat is heavier than the ammonia storm whipping
the great eye of Jupiter.
Noon of siesta when a desert town is shuttered and a brown-nippled
wife stretches out waiting for her husband, skin honey'd with sweat.
Noon of New York lunch break, Haitian taxis honk, and
Dominican luncheonettes where merengue muzak jingles over *platanos*
bubbling in water, and hamburger patties fry, while a blue-shirted cop
picks his teeth on the sidewalk.
That sun round as a woman with child nine months—
that is my enzyme.

If I could make noon into song it would be in the key of yellow
and played on a harpsichord dropped from the Capital Records building.
In noon were a poem: two Moorish girls bathing in the
Guadalquiver, and rumors of a ship at sea and a horse on the mountain.

To be born at dawn—a soul of an apple kept long in the refrigerator,
and chopped sweet for two lovers to devour.
To be born in the afternoon—an ox would struggle within me.
Born at night—what purple hounds leaping in my heart and biting
the memory of a girl's first breasts.
To be born in the dead of night—I could have ripped my stars
from fate.

But I was born at noon!
Absolute dreamer I am
born under the unwinking sun
at the hour when dogs bark
and no sane man answers.

FOR A FREE UNION

Every pregnant woman has moved to a different neighborhood,
every apple has been eaten by a shadow with teeth,
every shore I kiss has been claimed by the hyena,
every prophecy the hag coughs out of her lung-bag of phlegm,
every cantina has been ravaged by ivy,
every republic is a jungle where elephants rot,
every corn husk houses the locust;
but I continue cracking bones shaped like a wish,
I make mountains out of dust on the window sill,
I turn ash into clay and plant seeds under the skin of ice,
I rip the stone's stomach to find an island of pineapple and peach,
I fly through the mirror and land where light illumines the deepest cave,
I grow at the speed of crystal,
comprehend the poetry of amoeba,
open the bird cage where a cloud gives birth to a feather,
and summon the telekinesis of the ant;
but every power I have
wears away like lead in the pencil—
and though I bite my words,
though I whip them,
only a raccoon pauses from his labor,
then continues sniffing a milk carton and hot dog.

CONDUIT OF RAIN

I stick my tongue into
the center of your sex
     and taste

night milk, liquid forest,

wood sweating smoke,

honey tanned on the stomach of summer,

kelp twisted in the hair of a drowned man,

garden dripping from the fingers of dawn,

blood, apples, and suffocated air,

brine, garlic, and

while I eat,

your cries:
louder than
crickets or
timpani of the moon.

LIKE A JUTTED TOOTH I STOOD

It had rained all night, and the morning asphalt was slick and black as oil, as steam slowly rose in the blue morning heat. I was walking down to *avenida 16* to get a plate of *chilaquiles* and some coffee at a diner where no tourists ate. Soon I would pass *avenida Juárez* where the men mopping the bars would splash buckets of soapy water into the gutter, and on the sidewalk where puddles of dried vomit the texture of stale bread and oatmeal had been coughed from drooling mustaches.

There was no traffic yet, so I walked in the street in order to avoid the cans, laceless sneakers, and wet scraps of newspapers that littered the sidewalk. I walked past the concrete park with its benches crayon-stained with profanities, a fate enclosing a gut-twist of sewage pipes that hummed, and the gazebo painted five different shades of red where teenage couples would give each other purple blossoms of love on their necks. There was only an old woman dressed in a black shawl outside; she swept the gravel and dust from her sidewalk of dirt. Soon, the men would make their truck engines turn over with a groan; soon the children would ride their bicycles with stray neighborhood dogs chasing after them.

I was just passing the local laundromat when I bumped into a rope hanging in the middle of the street. It was apparently hanging from something up on high which I couldn't see because of a few remaining clouds. The rope was woven from steel wire—the thickness of two wrists—very much like the cable which holds an anchor, yet the bottom of the rope was frayed and missed the ground by an inch. I didn't know what to think, as I stared at the rope still swaying from my knocking into it. I tilted my head up, and yelled: *¿Se encuentra alguien allí arriba?* But there was no answer. Fearing I was the subject of a prank, I looked all around me for half-hidden faces in windows, on roof tops, under cars; for some reason which I still can't figure out, I even looked under my feet.

Not a soul. I pushed the rope, it swayed. I grasped it and lightly pulled it, but it didn't give. Realizing that I was the protagonist in what was developing into an allegory—but this was a *real* one—I tugged at it with considerable weight, and swung from it as if it were a liana. And the rope gave. Balancing myself back on my feet, I formed my hands into circles and felt the rope slide and accumulate into a pile the shape of a coiled hose around my feet. Though I was scared, I couldn't move; I wanted to know. Looking up at the clouds—the morning began to turn gray—I saw a black speck hurtling down. Slowly, the shape began to come into focus: it seemed to have a long neck and legs, yet I couldn't make out its size.

A shadow grew around the coil of rope that had bound my feet, then my ankles, and finally my knees. Because I couldn't move, I surrendered any hope of escape, and decided to study the object's descent. Once it was only several hundred feet above me, and spinning like a downed fighter plane, I saw a mane and tail, hooves, and even thin lips stretched over square teeth. Instinct shocked my nerves with panic, and I braced myself.

What I felt is similar to one in an economy car at a red light being rear-ended by a semi traveling at 80mph. I felt bones rip through my skin, my knees buckle and snap, and a dense liquidity pour into my lungs and gurgle up my throat. All this happened in a prolonged second below time before blackness swallowed me.

I came to under terrible pain and a drizzling sky the color of a bruise. A jalopy honked and clanked over the half-paved road, then made an ostentatious circumvolution around beast and crushed rider. A woman stuck her head out of the passenger window and screeched ¡estúpido! My body was numb; two glassy eyes stared at me, yet the muzzle didn't snuffle. The flies had already started to buzz when the rain began to fall.

THE CORK WHICH FLOATS ON WATER
IS CONSUMED BY FLAME

At two o'clock in the afternoon, sunlight and heat ripen on the thighs of schoolgirls in knee-length socks and mini-skirts. Through the school gates they walk when the city is drugged by siesta, and the strings of a lyre melt over the fire of my mind. Bus fumes rise and dissipate. From the sidewalk, I stare at those creatures the age between the smooth pubis of girlhood, and a seashell bedded in seaweed. My skull splits open as pigeons drop from gargoyles to peck at my spilled seed. No trees grow in this city, and at each corner the schoolgirls disappear like shadows erased by the wind. Soon they will no longer look over their shoulders, and a black bus will carry me over a road that rises through deserts and burnt mushroom fields. For now, there is no other hemisphere where I can catch the butterflies She shakes off her breasts upon awaking. But rain floods the basement of each poem I write. I step across these hot coals to not walk on water.

GRAVEL

Not everything is tundra. At times when I speak, the cloud under my tongue dissolves and leaves the taste of mint. When I sing, thorns never pierce my soles, chaparral blows through me, and the wind is my preferred velocity: I pass over arctic sheets, then over mist covering trees where monkeys screech, just by uttering a crisp consonant, or the long stomach of a vowel. After, my mouth full of rain, and all that remains of earth is the patch under my feet, and the horizon falls like a tower of ash. Then coffee and despair sudden as a leap-year, razors digested, and I appear on the street, where a taxi rips through the echo of a clearing in the forest. I return to my tundra where gravel flurries from swollen clouds and newspapers scurry in the wind, spreading the word.

LICK & SEAL

Herr Death has it in for me.
He rents the house next door where a Doberman sleeps under the awning,
  perks ears when I walk by, hunger rumbling in his throat.
Herr Death: nails manicured and shoes so polished no dust-lick of a Juárez
  summer will ever baste that black leather.
When we pass each other on the street and I'm on my way to the corner
  store for a quart of *Carta Blanca* and he's off to the Pentecostal
  church were amplifiers crackle funk gossip to sweet Jesus, he steps
  into the street, leaving me sidewalk shade.
At night I go for a stroll if a poem is not cracking a walnut shell *and* smoking
  a cigar, and pass by his window to spy on him asphyxiating
  hamsters in sealed plastic bags—though he never looks up he
  knows I'm watching.
Better are the letters he writes to me, all in *terza rima*, about Tuscan rose
  gardens, and the mopped floors of Heaven Towers.
But at night those rhythms & rhymes unravel in my sleep and black flak
  blasts, and the dust-spiders under my bent mattress rustle alive.
I wake up sweating enough to water all the vineyards in Northern California.

When Herr Death discovered through neighborhood wives gossiping in
  slippers that I like Thai, sure enough he was there at the *Peppered
  Shrimp* of Bangkok one day, eating my favorite lemon chicken,
  paperback of *Faust* in front of him.
Then I switched my lunch breaks to a hot dog stand and he materialized
  into the Mexican woman who slopped mustard & chili—I could
  tell by her blue eyes and the white steel slicing her English.
I do admire him—he always knows how to find me.
And always spiffy with suit & tie, shaved clean, no whiskers bristling under
  his chin.
But at night when the phone rings and I'm tired of hearing him imitate a
  graduate student doing sex calls for her food & gas,
and then the next day when my woman tells me: You had your chance, I
  called you but you never answered,
and then when I do answer, it's Herr Death asking: How 'bout a game of pool?

Just last week he was playing pool with my best friend at *The Blue Shore*,
  and over the click of balls rolling on green cloth, he bought us
  pitchers, offered cigarettes, and putting his arms around me, said:
  Don't worry.

And that remark leaves me in front of the typewriter where I pound visions
of mustard gas death, and E.coli spread like mint jelly on boiled
lamb, and an African rhino shaking the quiet of my street and chasing
me as the local men watch and spit, and car crash death, my front
teeth nailed into the steering wheel, gasoline choking my lungs, and
emergency surgeons sewing a tire and broken stereo into my stomach.

But Herr Death winks at me when I lock my door in the morning, as if
saying, don't be a poor sport, you have days, many days for washing
dirty laundry, and eating bread.
And your sentence will arrive in a letter addressed to you in your own writing,
dropped inside an envelope licked & sealed long ago.

THE VOYAGE UP NORTH

Listening to the couple screw next door is tasting ice on the polar cap, it is a kite-string hooked into my chest and dragging me up where stars crumble as I soar past them. At night, that couple floats down a river, and their voice slides up my bedroom walls the way a passing car wheels light over my ceiling. Listening to that couple screw is tumbling from the blues into a street where panthers leap up red skirts, and the air stinks of burped brandy, where I see a soldier, his arm slung around a woman's waist. They mount the stairs of a hotel, and I follow the two up to a floor with dusty tiles traversed by footprints which vanish at shut doors. The soldier and woman have long cut anchor, while I roam down the hall, listening to lovely animals migrate up north, on beds lofty as ice floes, as I row them to that thawing polar cap.

FABLE OF A WOLF, A LYRE, & ONE MILLION INHABITANTS

to Emilio Martinez

Listen my brother
About the ugly city
All the tarpaulins concealing bones and bent nails
And the acacias rotten and the pigeons
Crapping on the statue of Benito Juárez
The avenue through the desert
Where the wolf dumps the gutted women
And the wind gagging on dust
And the fat
Heat lolling under awnings, sucking shade
Oh my friend my brother
The world could fit in a crystal bowl
But still there would be windows to smash
Yet the sour light in August
Does not botch the singing
Of your drunkenness
Brother there are crows in our joy
And the vinegar of your verse
The tumbleweed scampering down *Calle Cobre*
And the litter
And the wind-swept, bursting
Scraps of litter!

After Kenneth Patchen

TO HIS MISTRESS THREE HOURS PREGNANT

Now the jungle prowls,
now the river sits up in bed to read this
tablet smashed on the sheets:

"the beetle rolling dung is Duke of Angkor Vat,
the jackal is Lord of Ninevah;
papyrus hendecasyllables of Archílocus
are gauze on mummified Alexandrians;
the jade of Tenochitlan
is chlorophyll for a sunken forest...
                              the drumming has stopped.
The flutes have been snapped..."

In this bed we stylus'd
glyphs on a star-silvered stomach,
and spat milk in the cave where the moon sweats.

Now clay blooms,
now meat stirs awake to chew
with slow-chapt jaw what
a man & woman have forged—

an Acropolis of smoke,
a rose garden in the arctic zone.
Lava raining on
palm trees and lianas, while above
vapor trail and a burst...

this pilot falls to us
because his
wings were ripped

LAST NIGHT, WITH THE UPSTAIRS

Newborn bawling, the laundry
flapping on the line, roaches breeding
news of light from antennae to antennae,
and the crimson arras glimpsed from
fire of sleep, I lay
after twelve hours of work & no bread,
heard jackals yelp by the river
where the shades
return with gospel of impossible Babylon...

THE RÍO BRAVO

No one rests at the bank of your palsy, wrinkled skin of water: dreg-juice of balsamic vinegar, coffee ground clogged in motor oil. Man charters your bleed in concrete; but where are your sylvan arbors, your green shade of Sundays in white linen? Your prophecy scooped from a basket of maize? No boy bathes in your water, nor leads oxen of mercy to haunch-splash tresses of water braided in bluest heat of noon, while two clouds fleck the sky, pushing the sky further South. Darker than the den of the tarantula, brown in which the ripped fetus floats, you trickle beneath the Santa Fe Bridge of stilting legs, bumper-to-bumper rattle of trucks, a rust-squeeking cinder of brakes, and you moisten no root, nor give drink to lipless teeth. All your fish have flitted into air, vanishing like spermatozoa that never reached the brilliant egg. And at night, no one sleeps at the bank of your waters. The moon-slick evaporates from your surface like exhaust fumes, while blackness stabs you, hilt-deep, and ants awaken.

DAWN IN DOWNTOWN JUÁREZ

Light absorbs darkness: a sponge sucking the hacked purple of a cow lung, and the glisten of a candied cherry on a porcelain plate. Young men dazed from having drunk pickled cactus juice in night clubs, start cars, or begin the long walk home. Cougar-blooded women with words venemous as hot bacterium, in crimson skirts, discover their shadows way-sided in the windows of all-nite diners and tripe-stew kitchens, then mount taxis bumbling like termites in the nest of mating. Here, dawn rips open boxes from which the leather shadows of crows flee prophecy, it scampers in the gutters and crackles in neon, pulls down the shades of ash, and oozes in the odor of wet wool, unwashed crotch, and milk curdled and belched. The morning wind knocks down memory, and the arches of drunkenness stain black, inverted rainbows under the eyes of the bedlamite.

SAYING GOODBYE TO CARTHAGE

I must go now.

I snip this cord of acetylene,
I mount the horse of sulfur and hydrogen,
dispatch telegrams of frost-crusted roses to the desert,
sink in a goblet of sky, braid
hair of the wind, dabble
with explosives that taste like tamarind,
and vomit the elasticity of milk &
pour the blue syrup of siesta.

I will pack my bags and wait at the platform
for the train that roars through the fireplace,
and sleep the long journey to
the attic where
lyres are tuned and all dogs happy.

I must leave.

My skein of blood unravels through another border.
Goodbye to the skins of wine I kissed,
goodbye to the hot grottos adrift in smoke,
goodbye to the women who never wrote me, the stars
that leapt under my skin, the shadows
rustling like silk when each door I opened
revealed breasts and cunt
turned into a pillar of iodine.
Once I felt the moon jump in my veins,
(I wrote a haiku about this but it got lost),
once I saw balloons released in a plaza
braided with the steam of meat and vendors,
once the water pipes clanked in the boarding house
while the city lit fireworks, and adulterers &
young lovers undressed in rooms jagged with crimson light,
(joy can easily fit in a bed with clean sheets).

But goodbye to your green and white taxi cabs,
I must depart.

Goodbye to your markets where trays
of meat stink the canned burn of menstruation, goodbye
to your produce of severed love, your beauty
of slit foreskins on a pushcart at noon, wasps churring,
goodbye to your recesses of marble & gold faucet bathrooms.

The desert gains another inch,
and there is no hay to harvest. Hard skies portend
the blue edge of nightmare will cut your dreams,
botch your autopsies,
and toss an appendix in the almoner's cup.
Because I deny your watermelons and dust,
(I couldn't care less),
I cut all strings never attached, and say
goodbye to your gymnasiums and diners,
I foreclose this scrap of light,
crumble your cathedral with a pinch of salt.
Not a peso will be
sweat on interest accrued.

(I must leave now).

This assassin is hungry.

HUNGRY ANIMAL I'VE BECOME

With my nails I scratch at the green beneath mud, I drink rain which has yet to burst from the earth's center. In my room, clouds never roam—so, I hit the streets; cars huddle and then burst; the police van prowls past cantinas where men sip the same beer for hours, and cough up the ink of a signed contract. Night: dust snakes between the thighs of a woman in a rose-colored dress, and beneath the earth, that mole I have never seen sniffs out purple and blue neon. Across the street is a pool hall: I imagine the click of balls wagers a leather sack which holds the western wind. Over the bongos of strip clubs where palms grow and parrots chatter, I hear the chop of a taco vendor dissecting tripe. But even all the fire trapped in candy won't fill me. Though my nostrils expand with the ocean's sweat, that life I once knew by the shore will never bloom again. Downtown, by the plaza, I want to crumble to dust, and then to become drizzle with quenches the clay I'm waiting to become, while fur and feces smoulder under a pile of top-hats and corsets, just around the corner.

Y para todo eso solo se te dieron palabras,
verbos y algunas vagas reglas. Nada tangible.
Ni un solo utensilio de esos que el refriegue
ha vuelto tan lustrosos. Por eso pienso que
quizás—como a mí a veces—te hubieses gustado más pintar.

—Carlos Martínez Rivas

(And for all this, they gave you words,
verbs, and some vague rules. Nothing tangible.
Not a single utensil that heavy usage
has turned so bright. For this I think
that perhaps—like myself at times—you would have rather painted.)

ON DE KOONING'S *WOMAN I*

Oh woman smeared in grease, brush-strokes of red,
blue of uncooked meat, saffron, the black
of fingernails after a day spent rebuilding
a carburetor, scooped out and scribbled on canvas
edges. He painted your skin all the luster
of lard, spat rouge only on your nose,
no nipples on your breasts, plastic bags
once filled with soda water now sucked dry.
But through that mess you smile—
five fangs chiseled dull as horse teeth—
you flaunt over your bite, saying:
what if you stick your tongue out at me,
I'll bite! And your eyes, the mud basins
of the Mississippi, yet wide open, glaring
at the one who had the nerve to paint you.
The leather shining on a General's
boots would not make you blink.
With a shopping bag in your right hand,
a clothes-iron in your left, you're armed lethal,
ready to wrestle all of Manhattan's taxis. Fueled
with Kentucky moonshine, you look me
in the eye the instant before you open
the crystal door to Saks Fifth Avenue.
And you're ready for a bargain, you're thrilled
to live on credit. Your feet, goat-hooves,
click in midair.

JACKSON AND THE BLACK DRIP

At last you abandoned the prairie
wastes, Diesel trucks, mud potholes,
and awe for Benton's Americana
thrown up from a dirt-bowl stomach—
and you breathed. With Siquieros, you saw
scarlet & sun in his spiral-
ing men of revolution, then dived
into the enzyme fury of your
mind, as you dipped a lacquer-
stiff brush into pints of beige,
pink, quince, and even chewed glass to
shrapnel onto canvases. You swirled paintings
which blinded eyes—
Autumn Rhythm, Gothic, and Full
Fathom Five! You painted
wind which blows through heart
and gut, deep as a bite
into a lover's neck, or a boy spurting
milk at the firmament. But after
fast cars, wake-up sweats and
buckets of whiskey splashed into your
liver, there were no more colors
to wrench from your mind. Over canvas tacked
on the studio floor, you black-widow'd
your soul, and before the dawn when
your Cadillac smashed against the pre-
ordained oak, you had only this:
from bourbon lungs your inspiritus
spinning in a smokewebbed night.

VERMEER

Even the dust and spear of straw on the kitchen floor are visible. The milk-maid pours a silken thread, clotted at the pitcher's mouth. On the table, loaves of wheat bread varnished by the gold of memory, while she gazes down at her chore, muscles around her elbows straining from the pitcher's weight. Behind her is a white wall, yellow-spotted, with one nail and its microbe-thin shadow. Outside the canvas, I only have patience to paint a nude with three brush strokes, but Vermeer includes the stitches on his maid's mustard-colored blouse. And he brings me back to slow light drifting after love, when her black hair burns against the white pillow, he brings me back to a boyhood afternoon where I sit by a window, feel sun on my back, and watch dust-specks pirouette in a weightlessness older than the first apple falling from the bough.

SKY CANVAS

With my tongue, I lick blue on this canvas. I paint herds of clouds, words heavy as bison, and a hunger for meat on rainy days. When I do not stretch the skin of the horizon, I peel oranges, and listen to the traffic of this city without trees. But when I write I see the woman who hides behind the sun. Birds come back to me, fish dart in my song, and I dance in a greener light while feeding on yellow colors.

ON *THE VOYAGE* BY MOTHERWELL

Days parched with olive and thistle, days of bone-white sky and bronze sand. One night—and once only—the moon rippled on the surface of a lake. In the middle of the journey, there was a mountain, and a river running through soil. But there were no orchards with the Lord's shadow, and the vision of a falling star left the taste of hickory on lips. Ochre dunes rippled like silk skeins for many moons until we reached a temperate valley. And it was there we learned to wait for centuries while torch lights flashed across chamber palace walls, and wind creaked the weather vane.

ON *THE FLOOR SCRAPERS* BY CAILLEBOITE

en attendant le bain dans la mer, a midi
—Rimbaud

All three are shirtless, with skin griddled over ribs. While working in the emptied parlor, they take swigs from a bottle of wine. They scrape and reveal the milk-meat of wood, as when my wife takes off her bra, and I see blue-white breasts and purple aureoles in moonlight. The mousse of wood-curls accumulates as two of the workers thrust heavy, iron scrapers against the oak floor. Outside, black umbrellas bloom as a cloud drowns the sun, and drops of rain pellet cobblestone. The city is an antcrawl of top hats, buggies, and bustles. Inside, the three men scrape until, hours later, the sun resurfaces and melds honey and chlorophyll. The floor scrapers wipe their brows, brush off their knees, and stretch. Time for cheese and bread, swigs of tart red, then, worn-weary with sweat, to bathe in the icy, noon-time river.

ON MODIGLIANI'S PORTRAIT OF DIEGO RIVERA

Corpulent and jocund, you grin
in a mahogany parlor the color
of a gourmand's coil of excreta
after a feast of steak and Merlot.

Your melanin glows in red-
earth the texture of chitin. Now you chuckle,
like the face of an omnibus passenger
half-riant behind the jerky window frame.

Why? Because you are gorged
with the sap of the pimp,
with the honey of the pentecost,
with bedroom eyes of Buddha,
with the burp of a lecher sated after his lunch...

And despite murals raised above factories,
colors mixed in denim and steel,
colors to eviscerate the pipes of capitalism,
despite the happy mustache of Stalin,
you were, and are in this portrait, a playboy
in heat, well-dressed, and piggish.

AFTER MOTHERWELL

The face of night is not
always black;
behind its shut eyelid, under
its ripped tongue, beyond
its mouth which sucks the gravity
of collapsed stars, there is
a streak of ochre,
there is a wink of scarlet like
flesh under the nail,
there is at last
a rupture and black froths and
spindrifts and swallows that light again,
but there was a
tumult and red streaked
across its face with
the profanity of brilliance.

ALL THINGS INCHOATE

MESSAGE SENT WHILE STARING OUT A BUS WINDOW

Like bubbles asphyxiating
in a glass of dead water,
the rain
shimmers on my aisle window.
The bus accelerates,
and the lane markers, white
lasers zipping into one
indivisable blur.
                    Over the hills,
a roiling ink-ooze of mist,
purple of clotted blood. The rain
has eaten the snow, thinned
whiteness to bald
patches of prairie shrubs the dun
of baked dung.
                    All of us, passengers
traveling at the speed
limit on the surface of this orb
wracked by solar winds, ultra-
violet light, and the shimmy of meteors.
                                    And yet,
newspapers are unfolded, the sun
opens her doors. I think: *one of these*
passengers must have seen mimosas
shiver. One of these women,
perhaps that brunette curled in sleep,
carries an egg the blue
of lit propane, where a helix un-
ravels a new tree of blood, a new
foliage of thought.
                    So does the dawn of lightning,
ever since the humid reign of
amoeba and kelp, blow
this species on course: like a
blurred lane marker glimpsed
through a moving window, in
a galaxy wrought of dark
matter with filaments so thin
that a million braided
would comprise but
one rung on the helix of DNA.

TO MY UNLIKELY READER

You, now in the Yucatán
isthmus where flies drone
over a skinned cow,
vats of milk simmer,
and a great-hipped woman
in a white cotton dress
slaps in sandals down
a street where iguanas sun
bathe, and shade
ripens green where
the old sit toothless,
and jabber like crickets.
                              You,
a girl of fourteen years,
breasts yet the size
of two peaches fallen on grass,
cotton-soft teeth, and skin
an aroma of boilt honey
wafted from a kitchen where
a woman guts chickens.
You, barefoot, half-
naked in hand-me-down shorts
a washed-out yellow,
rocking in a hammock in
an empty room painted
the blue
of currents that comb
the hair of the drowned
Phoenician sailor;
you with eyes
opening/closing in drawn
out gill-breaths of a shark
on the ocean floor.
                      For you
I write this:
               hibiscus sap,
blood in the swollen
prick itching for the coiled-hair conch,

coolness of shade at noon,
resiliance of milk,
the miracle of water;
I write for you
lavender mist of my mind,
damask rose of reverie, you
who now breathes and dreams;
I shape you from clay
and hot mud so that
a daisy stem snaps and
sprents juice on soil,
blood spots snow,
bull's-eye aches for arrow,
sand yearns for sierras,
nail pierces palm, so that
my breath brushes your feet & thighs,
billows your shorts, inhales
your naked breasts, neshes you
in sun, warmth, and will
whisper you sonatinas
of oranges
pianolas
wrist watches
mirrors,
all that is
inchoate, inchoate,
& never becoming.

I PONDER MY YOUTH UPON REACHING THE SMOKEWEBBED KIMMERIAN LAND

You had to end up where a bog stews against the horizon. All for an argosy rotting in your brain, and that homestead of withered poinsettia in a region of dunes. Glory still-born, and with undescended testicles. Words, like snapped lances. Look how the owl shakes off dust, and the sky is burnished indigo, clotted with mist, so that the waning moon is whetted into bull horns and gorges the liver of twilight, before black oozes, and silence gells.

INTO THE FURTHEST ORBIT OF MY LIFE

life is elsewhere

To glimpse a Uranian-glaze of blue
frozen methane
against the snow during moon-
lit hours when clouds
dredge
monotonous calcium.
        To open my front door,
and arrive at a vista
palpable as
a plum adrift in a black vacuum,
and self-hoodwinked, make
believe that the sun is
a red smudge slightly bigger
than the other stars
in a black sky with a scarce
atmosphere of helium,
a stroll on Pluto's moon, Charon.
        At least that
would ravel
in negatives of the
ferry lolling over currents where
torsos, breasts, and genitals writhe
in stygian crimson,
as steam rises, and the hull creaks.
        But here,
in the sierras,
the soul feeds on lumber
yards and railroad rust. Right now,
a truck lumbers through
billows of snow-haze.
Right now, the train passes,
cauterwall stabbing
the miles and the
freeze in between.

WHEN SINGING DOESN'T HAVE TO BE A SONG

A fat boy wearing a baseball cap, and a thin boy dressed up in regalia of boots and *Tejano* hat. The fat one carried a guitar with only three strings, but his fingers clawed the shape of a chord on the neck while he strummed a waltz. Like the sound of a crate dragged over gravel. Over this accompaniment *fortissimo*, the other boy straddled his boots on the floor, as if deftly astride on two galloping stallions, and sang. His melody was of a muezzin, a slithering of half-notes and pentatonic scales, like the music cats yowl in the blaze of summer nights. He sang ballads of mustachioed men fresh from urinals and flowing spigots of steaming beer. Men who skin calves. Men who sing of roses skewered on barbed wire, who dig up their notes from the bowels, and curse their old ladies who have gone up and left them for another man, from a different ranch. When that ballad was done, the guitarist began strumming again, and the singing resumed.

All this I heard and saw at a *torta* stand in downtown Juárez. You could buy a sandwich there for 6 pesos: two grilled weenies, American cheese, a slice of ham, jalapeño and avocado. I listened while I ate. Two tourists gave the boys a dollar after the second song. Or maybe two dollars. Maybe they even applauded. What matters, though, to the hands that sculpt, or to the ears that heard a nightingale sing, or to the eyes that found a scrap of lost dactyls, is how the accompaniment was ugly, but unfaltering, and how the boy sang—futilely perhaps—for gold or beauty, as does a diver delving deep into black water for a pearl, or a sharecropper for his withered fields, at the apex of the dog days.

THE CREEDENCE CLEARWATER REVIVAL

On the juke,
resinous of milk cleansing tar—
to hear
them croon in
a Juárez pool hall, 40 ouncer
Carta Blancas popped
and chugged, where
maquiladores drank.
To listen to that song,
far from the Pacific,
with my unqualified
loneliness of a 23 year
old staring at a dark
woman in an *S-mart*
cashier's vest,
enshrouded in blue
halo of cigarette smoke,
singing along about the rain, she
the announced whose
melody I did not hear,
though my ears
are still
ringing.

ON JUÁREZ CANTINAS, THE BEST AND WORST OF

The *avenida 16 de septiembre*: a sledgehammer of dust and sun to the brow. Brown clouds of bus fumes would rise and dissipate into a white sky flecked with blue. And the wood door, carved with nymphs, of *El Recreo*, a cantina that divided heat from the coolness of damp clay. The mahogany bar where men drank brandy and soda water. Postal workers on break, retired customs officers, teachers who would call in sick to watch TV beneath the whir of fans, to hear the pop and fizzle of beers opened and poured into chilled glasses. A perpetual half-light with freshness of sheets, still damp from the wash, flapping on the clothesline. The *cantinero* would stare at clients with his lidless eyes of an ancient tortoise. Shoe shiners would rag-burnish boots until they gleamed like an oil slick. The clack, clack, clumber of dice shook and tumbled on the bar. And the sweet smell, like a breeze rattling parched weeds, of rice paper cigarettes lit, mixed with phosphor, and dissipated in billows of fanned air.

At night, when thirsts would scatter like ants, and *El Recreo* had closed, there was *La Puerta Azul*. After hours, a *cantinero* would size up the shadow-enveloped figure through the door opened a crack, and, if it was safe, usher him inside from the night, with its prowling cop cars. Mirrors above the bar, on the wall behind the barstools, doubled the gold, mint, and clear syrup of liquor bottles. Men in *Tejano* hats, brims down and furtive, stirred their brandies. In the booths, musicians dressed in black smoked, while outside, the dawn would bleed violet on the jagged-toothed billboards, antennae, and storefronts.

Or *El Bombin* in the red-light district, with pissy urinals, walls painted sea-green, and the nausea of truckers, factory workers, and women with silver teeth, all adrift in a haze pungent as cigar-smoke. Or the cantinas with splintered, swiveling doors and concrete floors, wherein men would stagger while the juke crackled with the wheeze and polka-beat of norteño ballads. All of those grottos, flesh sucked of blood, sour thirsts served the acid of neon.

And the last alley cantinas: square, submerged cells stuffed with cologne and sweat, and shifting brown waters.

MEZCAL

Galeguetza carnival, Oaxaca;
midnight in the zócalo

After the red
spider of thirst
scratched
down my throat
& wove
his web of acid,
I drank a bottle.
The salt film before
my eyes
peeled;
shadows turned to smoke,
a blood-stream of color
sprayed
in the boom
of fireworks,
the faithful
raised
bottles while
fingers of xylophone
dug
into my eyes,
plucked daylight
from memory,
& unblinded,
I stumbled by
the Zapotec women who
genuflected
before a tree,
poured draughts
of clear mezcal for
man-root,
woman-fish,
and the prodigal dead.

AFTER TAKING A DEEP BREATH

I left north for the mountains.

My glass of wine had turned to vinegar.
I swept the attic that creaked in my skull,
then dredged salt on the wood floor & heard
sodium hiss in
the silvery tracks left by words
that had once cocooned in synecdoches.
I listened to the chlorine sizzle
the last miniscule
puddles of plasma, like the sound
of slick asphalt under the tires of a sports car.

I lay down
on a mattress, & folded my faith over my chest, yet
all I could image was a tea-cup brimming over with sand.

It was then I heard
the storm banging on the five doors
that harbor my blood, and regulate
my floodgate of language. The door
of the ears with which I hear water
thrumming in the lungs of a blue sailor;
the basement door to my mouth
flooded with sunlight;
the door always unlocked, meaning my eyes;
the portal of ossified blood, my penis; &
my fingers,
doors double-locked ten times although
they unhinge the windows of ice.

The storm whirlpooled
with the noise that the shepherd heard on a night
when phosphor whistled in red air, & fire rained
on the sinking keel of a citadel.
And the storm entered my language
with a crackle of dry thunder,
with the tenacious hunger of a maggot, &
the suffocation of black rubber, yet
my window shutters remained locked.

I left the south and its fauna.

The vendor who stirred sugar & melon juice
into vats of water, while the summer burned.
The woman with kinky black hair &
breasts heavy with moonlight & cool water who
taught me the art of strict pleasure in an unswept
room that echoed the noise of the streets.
The evenings, and the men drinking on their porches.

It was only after many roads,
hundreds of words—too many—
that I arrived to this cordillera of thought.
This tundra
where the storm came & spoke to me.
Words bled through my eyes, they trickled
from my ears, smoked from my mouth,
like a cloud of ink muddying water:

have no faith in poets, poets
are a fluff of wet feathers in a cage,
yet poetry exists and buoys us as we
trace the blue current of a thought so that
shadows walk through granite,
great birds lift islands from the ocean floor,
and two lovers still green, or adulterers,
or husband & wife may take off
on beds with the wing-span of tall trees.

By then my shutters banged open.

The cabin of this poem was
awash with sunlit shafts of dust.
A single moth flew in circles.

From the door came
the wood-sweet smell of baked bread.
My hands unfolded, and I saw the glass
of wine empty, though no
finger prints glistened with transparency.

HE WAS A MAN

who dragged night
across a garden:
eyes bleared from drink,
boxer's shoulders
from hauling and
installing air conditioners,
and his woman
now pregnant,
trying to hook him into
marriage.
I stared at those two,
while we smoked & sat
on a park bench in Juárez.
White heat,
crowds milling,
and myself
their one friend
saying what a beautiful
baby it would be,
when he
surer than the scalpel's incision,
succinct as haiku,
pressed
the smouldering butt
against his calloused palm.

¿Qué nueva luz, qué clara maravilla
se aposentó en mi alma?

Dámaso Alonso

(What new light, what lucid wonder
lodged itself within my soul?)

ADZ

No wine here, only harpies licking the sweat off cheese.

I want the ebony sands of Rousseau, where lions will pass through my sleep, and the wind will pluck my zither.

But no nocturnes chiseled from shadow; the rustling of silk is ripped, the wax seal is broken, my mistress has turned into a column of smoke, and through the gold-leaf halls, an ammonia dust duns the scarlet river of Delacroix.

No pubis.

Only gravel shaken inside a skull.

No rhythm.

The gills of a fish choking on air.

No shape, no shoulders.

The skein of blood wound tight around the equator.

Only bread choking on sand.

Only the magnesium spider spinning his web.

But my drumming has started,

for an alchemy of denim and silk.

For a screech tantamount to Dante.

For sex heated in a spoon.

For all the sailors with the face of Jesus.

For oranges, jackals, marble, and shade.

Because the lilacs

have all withered in the Carolinas.

The woman carrying parasols are ghosts in the oils of Monet.

No parlors here, no sherbet.

Water sucked by cactus, bloody shit of coyote, accordian wheezing in C major, and vats of goat meat boiling in broth.

But an adz grows in my hand,

and I chop I

chop

chop

chop.

I chop the muscle that holds word and sense together.

I chop to savor water in two syllables, so that

the world ripens, apples bloom, beer becomes beer, birds become birds, and black is the secret ambition of whiteness.

DIPPING MY INFANT SON INTO THE BLACK RIVER

At times I want to file this cable
so that, adrift,
the white fingers of drowned ghosts
will wrap around you
and drag you across
coral red as demon-tongue into
a blankness beyond oxygen that
will seal over you, seamless.

Because my words that smell of wet kittens,
that ignite forests,
& slam a funnel up the drunkard
bent over, sucking on a severed crotch;
because the gifts I offer you,
a spikenard, a coffee bean, spit
in the palm, are nothing compared to
milk, the slow acid of moonlight, water
sweetened in a bucket of cedar, a plum...
though your world too will shrivel
into workers picking their teeth over a man-hole,
walls of stucco humming with pipes that
throw up the shit of millions into the sea,
two shirtless boys in Juárez
rolling a tire down a street,
elevators raising the obese,
and the desert crawling
the miles until it reaches your door.

And it is a door I can't open,
water rising, swallowing my ankles my waist,
when I see myself no longer,
an absence in the mirror, while
you shave and study your graying whiskers.
There are evenings awaiting you,
evenings stained with the ink of obituaries,
and nightmares submerged in shots of brown liquor.
But also walks in a gust of rain,
the wind talking nonsense, and rooms

hot with the nakedness of woman,
though all pleasures will bleed alkaline
long after sweetness bites your nipples.
                                        And yet suppose
soothsaying is the Ides that was not a danger,
and that these words
are the memory of what will never happen.
Because it is a butcher hook when I don't see you,
so that my veins are gutted and glisten
atop my skin, and are pulled
to the point of snapping,
and within my core
I feel entrails & pancreas ripped inside-out.
Do you feel my lips against your cheek?
It is a hunger to bite into the peach,
to singe its fuzz,
it is a hunger to be consumed,
to be the voltage of your enzymes,
to dive into the babble of your new tongue,
to drink the milk of your bones,
flit my life into yours,
and fell the gathering dark...
                            the hope you give is so heavy,
it could fit in a basket, and float.

TO THE READER

Whether or not
you speak of the grain
of oak bark weathered
the color of elephant;
or the stirring
of ants in a dead possum;
whether or not
you, a praise of flesh
through which the first word burns,
know the smokewebbed
canals of sleep;
                    you
brighter than a raised
glass of ale, you
sweet rankness of
roasted boar, you
greater than corn,
united with the wheat, you

are a voice,
a breath
carving the curve
of an O, blade
honing impossible sand
into the circle of water;

you are the fleeting
element between
stone & flint, and
red air
conjugated in the
third person singular.

TO MY TONGUE SECRETING HEAVY ICICLES

The brightest murder of crows
does not
stain this splendour
of petrified milk.
The page turns a shade paler.

The blackest spurt of doves,
harboring what skies
submerged in a mug of ale,
does not undo
the knotted cables of heat,
as ovaries blossom
miraculously where
the horned sun expected
a gall bladder to stink like cod.

The baldest eagle
whose crag of ripped granite,
wolf-fang of a false herbivore,
does not portend
brighter words where the
current is freezing, the plankton many.

But I in my green hour
when word and skin meld,
am but a tortoise
who pushes a sea with his beak,
and, a mild success,
munches kelp at the
dregs of a bluest voltage.

MORNING AGAIN

The trees on my street have stretched their arms, and dust, after a night of sleeping on rooftops, now scurries in the streets. Where are the children who splashed courtyards with blue songs? Where are the soccer balls and sandals? Last night I heard the children as I read the prose poems of Miguel Angel; tried to write, but an oil slick choked the tide, and the only kelp I tasted was in the fist of a drowned man surfacing at midnight. The children are all in school; even the dust has migrated. But the purple tint of smoke and memory leaves the taste of hickory on my lips. Take this daylight dipped in acid, but not these soluble words. I hoard verbs from the sharks that circle above me.

A MAP OF FOUR PILLARS
& A GLIMPSE OF THE OMNIPRESENT FIFTH

A MAP OF FOUR PILLARS AND A GLIMPSE OF THE OMNIPRESENT FIFTH

The city, with its stop signs and traffic signals is a construct of collective imagination. The driver stopping before a red octagon is reminiscent of the savage kneeling before a stone idol dreamed of and chiseled by his ancestors. In California, freeway signs announce approaching towns with such baroque appellations as Arcadia, Palos Verdes, Valencia—the grazing grounds for Daphnis and Chloe, rather than places where men and women drink coffee in the morning, and make love at night. Still, the driver in California never doubts that the desert dotted with turquoise and mauve townhouses is a natural oasis. Such is the power of language to convert a desert into a garden.

Although the traffic signal is a tool for the creative act of communication, it is only a sign. It is not a symbol: that indecipherable herald, that avatar of reticence, of things "half-withheld, have-given away," as Borges wrote in *Two English Poems.* The poem is made of the linguistic equivalent of the symbol, the metaphor: that fat Russian woman pulled out of a fat Russian woman; that chameleon which changes its colors when thrust under a different light; that beauty who once said "I love you", but in a different hemisphere, when the air was tinted blue with cigarette smoke, and a *cuba libre* was finished off with the finality of a general ordering an execution.

In a poem, each word becomes a pottery shard, its jagged edges testimony of the curved water jug before it shattered. The word insde a poem is a blow of an adz between signifier and signified; for a moment, a woman's sex can become an oyster on a platter of raw cow tongues, or milk-slush scooped out of an empty locust husk. Syllables become sounds, words both reveal and conceal what they wish to name, and reality, that concept whose definition depends on the time of day, is yet unnamed. For this moment below time, one walks in Eden, and consonants and vowels become promising as a belly round with child.

But the language of the newspaper is either sterile, or eroded, like monuments from crumbled civilizations: those Latinate words which fill the discourse of the politician, or the anemic vocabulary of the United Nations, or the words used as stones, or for religious dogma. Blake labeled such concepts as "truth", "God", etc., as "mind-forged Mannacles", and indeed it was he who, in "The Marriage of Heaven and Hell", wrote:

"The ancient poets animated all sensible objects with Gods or Geniuses, calling them by the names and adorning them with the properties of woods, rivers and whatever their enlarged & numerous senses could perceive till a system was formed by attempting to realize or abstract the mental deities from their objects: thus began Priesthood. Thus all men forgot that All deities reside in the human breast".

Although it is safe, even desirable, for urban traffic signals to function as signs where A=B, symbols open language to a degree where A=B, but also C, D, E, F... Such words as God, Allah, or Adonai, are but chinks that offer glimpses into that region where the wind is still green, clouds dissolve under the tongue, and a starfish floats in the heart.

One of the questions often asked of poetry is whether it can penetrate through this reality into another, or even better, be a map, a cosmological map, diagramming all the realms dreamt of at night, and lived during the day. Among the many metaphors which poets utilize to articulate this quest there comes to mind Borges' "aleph", or Whitman's all-inclusive "I" who is ego, soul, and Oversoul, all at once. True, not every poet attempts to fuse with the Oversoul, but one can set up a difference between versifiers and poets, and between poets and prophets (those who know that the poetic idiom, or symbolic language, can chart out another reality). Sarah Teasdale wrote lovely verse, Philip Larkin wrote wonderful poems, and Richard Wilbur, elegant ones, yet they do not come close to the idea of the poet as "vates", the Latin word for both poet and prophet. There are poets who write poetry which offers the reader, in the words of Alberto Blanco, "un mapa de cuatro pilares, vislumbre de la quinta omnipresente", or "a map of four pillars and a glimpse of the omnipresent fifth": Yehuda Amichai with his biblical *and* urban tone, Miroslav Holub—the scientist/poet—Allen Ginsberg's flowing cadence, Octavio Paz, Huidobro, Guillevic, Jerome Rothenberg, Joaquín Pasos, Reverdy, Yannis Ritsos, García Lorca, Lamantia, Amir Gilboa, José Gorostiza, Neruda, are only a handful of the poets who come to mind.

An important digression: one must remember that prophet does not mean fortune-teller; as Paul Portugés points out in *The Visionary Poetics of Allen Ginsberg*: "the reader should not be confused with the popular idea of a prophet as a magician, who can tell what's going to happen. Instead, the poet-prophet is a revealer of eternal truths, a seer—not the foreteller of the future".

When Le Comte de Lautreamont wrote his vision of beauty as the chance sight of an umbrella and sewing machine side by side on a dissecting table, he wrote a catalogue without logic, a maxim which imparts no pragmatic advice. And yet it is necessary, and has not been forgotten, but continues to remain not only the "first" surrealist metaphor, but one of the greatest visions ever seen in poetry. If poetry reveals how language is arbitrary, isn't there also the danger that poets are liars not only unworthy of entering Plato's Republic, but daily life as well? No. Poetry is not only the stuff of visions and prophecies, but of mud and wood, of rough hands and wool. A poem can be about a chariot seen in a vision; it can also be about a visit to the dentist, about dressing well, about the tedium of thinning hair, the depression which sinks in on Sunday afternoons, the sweet flavor of beer. Whatever poetry touches turns into something different than originally intended; a visit to the dentist, and all the pains therewith associated, becomes as heroic as Ajax's suicide. The frozen food and deli sections of a supermarket become the twisting halls in a neon labyrinth.

So, when one begins to say that poetry is prophecy, and that it is as mad as the sight of an umbrella and sewing machine on an operating table, and then in the next breath state how poetry can celebrate the moon, cucumbers, a bus-ride, shoes, the way a wife takes off her panties when she believes her husband isn't watching her, what does this say about making any attempt to speak intelligently about poetry? Just as symbols elude any one definition, so does poetry slip out of grasp the moment you feel it at your fingertips. If poetry were mystical only, what would we do with the urban, gossipy poems of Frank O'Hara? If the poetic idiom were only the long lines based on units of breath in Ginsberg's poetry, what would one make of the terse lines of William Carlos Williams? If poetry were in the iambic pentameter of Shakespeare, what of Robert Frost's iambic pentameter in "Birches" derived from the American vernacular? A poem can be a sonnet or a haiku, and yet a sonnet or haiku written as an academic exercise is not necessarily a poem.

Even worse, so far I have mostly celebrated poets who are known for a more "visionary" style, yet what about "plain" narrative poets? Is not George Crabbe an excellent poet? And what about Edgar Lee Masters? What about the crisis in genres? Is *Pedro Páramo* not only a novel, but an extended prose poem as well; or is it not only an extended prose poem, but a novel as well? How do we define Italo Calvino's *Invisible Cities*? At best, poetry is not about scanning feet, or about line breaks, or about vocabulary, and especially not about those charts and figures constructed by Formalists which look more like statistical reports on the effectiveness of Pap smears than anything to do with poetry. Certain words, certain combinations of words, in a verbal alchemy, become a poem. When the reasons on how and why are fully discovered, poems will no longer exist, or will be better than ever.

Although poetry can be prophecy, and although words in a poem function as symbols, the rhythm and intensity of "language charged with meaning" and the lightning-bolt flashes of metaphors are within the reach of every man and woman. Poetry is in the library, but it is in the streets as well.

One can arrive at a poem through drugs and sex, but also through meditation, or through doing "nothing". The language heard in the kitchen, the insults of taxi drivers, the struggles of a toddler making sentences as if they were mud pies, the salacious euphamisms and come-ons of prostitutes, the slang of rich teenagers and of hoods, are much closer to poetry than academic essays, newspaper articles, government propaganda, or monster deodorizer and fudge-based skin emollient commercials heard on the radio.

Jack Kerouac has never been read as a literary critic or theorist, yet when he defended his theory of spontaneous prose and of poetry based on sound, rather than sense, he dismissed the theory of the "objective correlative" as academic quibbling, but quickly stated that Eliot's poetry was "sublime." That is, poetry is not arrived at through theories about poetry; poetry is arrived at through, and only through, the writing of a poem. Words as symbols, poetry as prophecy, as a humble consolation for the heartbroken lover, as bread shared by everyone, as the visions seen in the book of Revelations, as seventeen syllables written about a frog leaping into a pond—every theory is valid as long as the result is a poem. One can't deny that personal taste and opinion have much to do with this, and that tastes are often erratic; I can easily live without the collected works of Alexander Pope, but Wyatt's "They Flee From Me" is as vital in my reality as water.

Poems sprout overnight, like those desert cities in California, with town houses all alike and painted the color of guava and watermelon, with fountains filled with goldfish, and with streets of wet-black asphalt, half-melted under a sun like a pendulum which no longer swings. On those streets, even though you are in what was once desert, you must stop at red octagons, and remember to let on-coming traffic have right of way before making a left. It is all a world wrought from imagination; like the poem, the city is made of words that elude meaning the instant they are defined.

—Anthony Seidman

ABOUT THE AUTHOR

Anthony Seidman lives with his wife and son outside Denver, where he is a Spanish teacher. He studied at Syracuse University and at the University of Texas at El Paso and lived in Mexico for four years. *On Carbon-Dating Hunger* is his first book.

The Bitter Oleander Press Library of Poetry:

The font used in this collection of poetry is the digital representation of a family of type developed by William Caslon (1692-1766). Printer Benjamin Franklin introduced Caslon into the American colonies, where it was used extensively, including the official printing of the *Declaration of Independence* by a Baltimore printer. Caslon's fonts have a variety of design, giving them an uneven, rhythmic texture that adds to their visual interest and appeal. The Caslon foundry continued under his heirs and operated until the 1960s.